THE SCIENCE OF

AIR

PROJECTS AND EXPERIMENTS WITH AIR AND FLIGHT

Bibliographical Note

TABLETOP SCIENTIST: THE SCIENCE OF AIR, Projects and Experiments with Air and Flight, first published by Dover Publications, Inc., in 2013, is an unabridged reprint of the work originally produced by David West Children's Books, London, in 2005. The text has been revised to conform to American vocabulary.

International Standard Book Number

ISBN-13: 978-0-486-49265-0
ISBN-10: 0-486-49265-6

Manufactured in China
49265601
www.doverpublications.com

TABLETOP SCIENTIST: THE SCIENCE OF AIR
was produced by

David West 👫 Children's Books
7 Princeton Court
55 Felsham Road
London SW15 1AZ

Designer: Rob Shone
Editor: Gail Bushnell
Picture Research: Gail Bushnell

PHOTO CREDITS :
Abbreviations: t-top, m-middle, b-bottom, r-right,
l-left, c-centre.

Pages 3, 4t & b, 16tl, 20tl, 22t, 24m, 28t – Corbis Images.

Every effort has been made to contact copyright holders of any material reproduced in this book. Any omissions will be rectified in subsequent printings if notice is given to the publishers.

With special thanks to the models: Meshach Burton, Sam Heming De-Allie, Annabel Garnham, Andrew Gregson, Hannah Holmes, Molly Rose Ibbett, Margaux Monfared, Max Monfared, Charlotte Moore, Beth Shon, Meg Shon, William Slater, Danielle Smale and Pippa Stannard.

An explanation of difficult words can be found in the glossary on page 31.

THE SCIENCE OF AIR

AIR

PROJECTS AND EXPERIMENTS WITH AIR AND FLIGHT

TABLETOP SCIENTIST

STEVE PARKER

DOVER PUBLICATIONS, INC.
Mineola, New York

CONTENTS

The air which makes our weather…

…is measured using scientific devices…

…and holds up airplanes too, so we can fly around the world. Air also fills our car and bike tires.

INTRODUCTION

Look all around you—what can you see? Not air, even though it *is* all around you! Air is invisible. When we "see" it, we are really seeing particles floating in it, like dust or water droplets. Or we are seeing its effects when it moves and blows, as the wind. Air might seem too light to have any weight. But it can be weighed and it presses on us with a surprisingly powerful force. Of course, without air there would be no wind, clouds or weather. Air is even inside you. We must all breathe fresh air every few seconds to stay alive. Scientists describe air as "a mixture of gases forming a compressible fluid," that is, air can flow and be squeezed smaller. Our scientific understanding of air means we can move it, push it, compress it, stretch it, alter it, measure it, and use it in countless ways, every day.

HOW IT WORKS

These panels explain the scientific ideas in each project and the processes that make it work.

Prepare each project carefully and follow the instructions. Remember: real scientists always put safety first.

TRY IT AND SEE

These panels show more ideas to try so you can experiment and find out more about air.

Where you see these symbols:

 Ask an adult to help you.

 Sharp tools may be needed.

 Project to be done outdoors.

 Prepare work surface for a messy project.

AIR ON THE GO

Air is rarely still. The layer of air around the whole Earth, called the atmosphere, is always on the move. It is heated by the sun and parts of it get less dense, or lighter. A "bubble" of warmer air rises above the cooler air around it. Some of this cooler air flows along to take its place causing winds to blow across the surface of Earth.

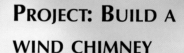

Hot-air balloons contain air warmed by a burner. It is lighter than the surrounding cooler air, so the balloon takes off.

PROJECT: BUILD A WIND CHIMNEY

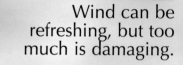

Wind can be refreshing, but too much is damaging.

WIND CHIMNEY

WHAT YOU NEED

- **large plastic bottle**
- **foam board**
- **aluminum foil**
- **thread**
- **drinking straw**
- **bead**
- **glue**
- **craft knife**

1. CAREFULLY TRIM THE TOP AND BOTTOM FROM A LARGE PLASTIC DRINK BOTTLE. AT ONE END, CUT OUT TWO SQUARE SHAPES OPPOSITE EACH OTHER.

2. CUT A CIRCLE OF ALUMINUM FOIL TO FIT INSIDE THE BOTTLE. TRIM AWAY TWO QUARTER-SEGMENTS. TWIST THE REMAINING SEGMENTS TO MAKE A FAN-SHAPE.

3. GLUE TWO LONG FOAM BOARD STRIPS OPPOSITE EACH OTHER AT THE OTHER END OF THE CHIMNEY FROM THE CUTOUTS. GLUE THE STRAW ACROSS THEIR ENDS.

UPS AND DOWNS

As air warms, its tiny particles, called atoms and molecules, move farther apart. There are fewer of them in a certain volume, so the warm air is lighter, or less dense, and moves upward. In the atmosphere, it is colder higher up. The air cools, becomes heavier, and sinks. This sets up a continual flow called atmospheric circulation.

PLASTIC BOTTLE CHIMNEY

RISING HOT AIR

FOIL SHAPE

COLD AIR

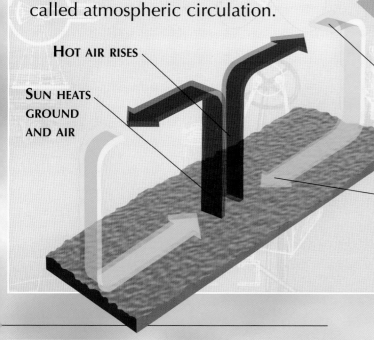

HOT AIR RISES

SUN HEATS GROUND AND AIR

HEAT SOURCE

HIGH UP, AIR COOLS AND SINKS

COOL AIR MOVES TO REPLACE HOT AIR

4

MAKE A SMALL HOLE IN THE MIDDLE OF THE FOIL. TIE ONE END OF THE THREAD TO THE BEAD. THREAD THE OTHER END THROUGH THE HOLE IN THE FOIL AND TIE IT TO THE STRAW.

TOWER POWER

ADJUST THE THREAD SO THE FOIL "FAN" HANGS NEAR THE BASE. PUT THE CHIMNEY NEAR WARM AIR, FROM A RADIATOR, HOT WATER BOTTLE OR SUNNY WINDOW. THE WARM AIR RISES UP THE CHIMNEY, PUSHES THE BLADES AND MAKES THEM SPIN. SCIENTISTS ARE PLANNING REAL "SOLAR CHIMNEYS" ON HOT DESERT SAND TO MAKE ELECTRICITY. THESE CHIMNEYS WILL BE OVER 1/2 MILE HIGH.

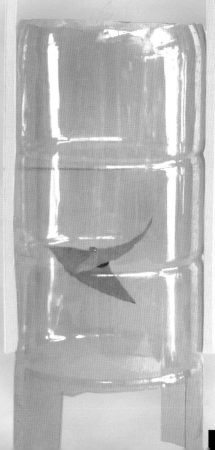

HOW WINDY?

How windy is it today? Is there a gentle breeze or a howling hurricane? Weather scientists, or meteorologists, need to know the detailed direction and speed of the wind. To measure these features they use a wind vane and anemometer.

The wind spins the cups of this portable anemometer, giving a digital readout.

PROJECT: MAKE A WINDSPEED METER

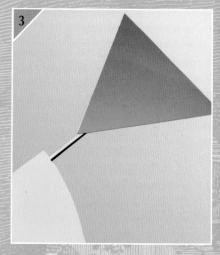
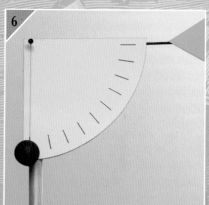

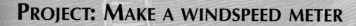

1 CUT A LARGE QUARTER-CIRCLE OF CARDBOARD. GLUE A THIN DOWEL ALONG ONE STRAIGHT EDGE.

2 GLUE THE CARDBOARD TUBE TO THE OTHER EDGE. TAPE CARDBOARD OVER THE TUBE END IN THE CORNER.

3 GLUE A CARDBOARD TRIANGLE TO THE TAIL OF THE DOWEL. THIS IS THE WIND VANE.

4 PUSH A THUMB TACK INTO THE CORNER OF THE CARDBOARD'S NON-TUBE SIDE. GLUE ONE END OF THE STRING TO THE PING-PONG BALL. TIE THE OTHER TO THE TACK.

5 DRAW EVENLY-SPACED LINES ALONG THE CARDBOARD'S CURVED EDGE. PLACE THE THICK DOWEL INTO THE GROUND SOMEWHERE WINDY. SLIDE THE TUBE OVER IT.

6 CHECK THE PING-PONG BALL SWINGS FREELY ALONG THE WINDSPEED SCALE AND THE WHOLE ANEMOMETER SWIVELS AROUND EASILY ON THE DOWEL.

WHAT YOU NEED

- stiff cardboard
- small tube
- thin dowel
- thick dowel
- string
- ping-pong ball
- thumb tack
- glue
- scissors

THE PUSH OF THE WIND

As the wind's speed rises, the ping-pong ball is pushed higher up the scale. Put numbers on the scale and take measurements regularly through the day. If the wind is gusty (variable), try to get an average reading during ten seconds.

FACE THE WIND

The moving air pushes on the broad, flat surface of the wind vane and makes it turn. It swivels until the wind's force on it is least—when it points directly downwind. In this position the anemometer's ping-pong ball faces directly into the wind, and there the push of the moving air is greatest.

WIND VANE

WIND

BE A "WINDBREAK." STAND ON THE UPWIND SIDE OF THE ANEMOMETER. DOES THIS CHANGE THE READING?

PING-PONG BALL

HEAVY PRESSURE

All substances have weight, even air. Its weight presses on everything, including our bodies. But we are so used to it we do not feel it. The pushing force of air is known as air pressure.

The pressure of the air around us is known as atmospheric pressure. It can be different in different places. Changes in atmospheric pressure are connected to the weather. On a weather map, a line drawn through places of equal air pressure is called an isobar.

As a pump is used to force more air into a car tire, the air pushes back with increasing pressure. Due to the extra air, the tire is also very slightly heavier.

PROJECT: BUILD

AN AIR WEIGHER

AIR WEIGHER

WHAT YOU NEED

- **foam board**
- **two plastic cups**
- **identical balloons**
- **thumb tacks**
- **glue/tape**
- **craft knife**
- **nail/pin**

1

GLUE A STRIP OF FOAM BOARD, THE STAND, TO A RECTANGULAR CARD BASE. GLUE SMALL FOAM BOARD TRIANGLES AT THE JOINT TO KEEP THE STAND UPRIGHT.

2

CUT ANOTHER LONG STRIP OF FOAM BOARD FOR THE BEAM OF THE BALANCE. CAREFULLY MAKE A SMALL HOLE EXACTLY IN THE MIDDLE OF IT.

3

FIX A PAPER CUP AT EACH END OF THE BALANCE BEAM USING TAPE, GLUE, OR THUMB TACKS. MAKE A SMALL HOLE IN THE CENTER TOP OF THE STAND.

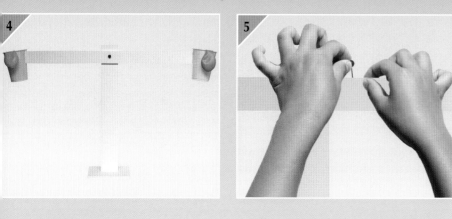

4

5

PUSH A LONG PIN OR NAIL THROUGH THE HOLES IN THE STAND AND BALANCE BEAM. THE BEAM MUST TILT FREELY. PUT A BALLOON IN EACH CUP.

ENSURE THE BEAM IS EXACTLY LEVEL. IF NECESSARY, ADD TINY WEIGHTS SUCH AS THUMB TACKS OR PAPER CLIPS TO THE SIDE OF THE BEAM WHICH IS HIGHER.

NO LONGER LEVEL

STEADYING THE BALANCE BEAM, REMOVE ONE OF THE BALLOONS FROM ITS CUP. BLOW IT UP AND PUT IT CAREFULLY BACK IN PLACE—AND DOWN GOES THE CUP! BEFORE, THE BALANCE BEAM WAS LEVEL. NOW IT IS NOT AND THE ONLY DIFFERENCE IS THE AIR IN ONE OF THE BALLOONS.

EXTRA AIR

Blowing up the balloon forces lots of air into a very limited space. As more air goes in, it tries harder to get out, and pushes on the inside of the balloon with increasing pressure. There is air pressure inside the other balloon, too, – but it's the same as the normal atmospheric pressure outside.

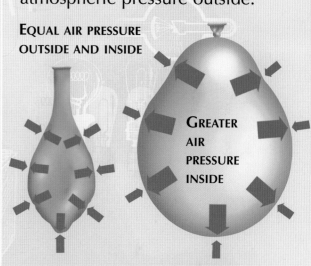

EQUAL AIR PRESSURE OUTSIDE AND INSIDE

GREATER AIR PRESSURE INSIDE

PARTLY BLOW UP THE OTHER BALLOON. DOES THE BALANCE BEAM TIP DOWN LESS?

PAPER WEIGHT

Smooth a sheet of newspaper over a ruler over-hanging the table. Quickly hit the ruler's end. It is mostly the weight of the air that stops the paper from rising.

TRY LARGE AND SMALL SHEETS, SMOOTHED DOWN CAREFULLY. WHICH MOVES LEAST?

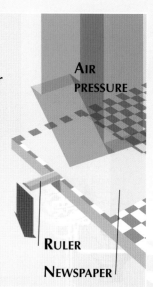

AIR PRESSURE

RULER

NEWSPAPER

MEASURING AIR PRESSURE

The air all around presses on us and everything else with a force called atmospheric pressure. This pressure does not stay the same. Changes in atmospheric pressure are linked to the weather. A barometer measures changes in atmospheric pressure to help us forecast the weather.

Barometers are used on ships to warn of high winds and storms.

PROJECT: BUILD A BAROMETER

BAROMETER

CUT OUT AND STRETCH A PIECE OF BALLOON OVER THE JAR. TAPE IT FIRMLY TO THE RIM.

TAPE ONE END OF THE DRINKING STRAW TO THE CENTER OF THE BALLOON CIRCLE.

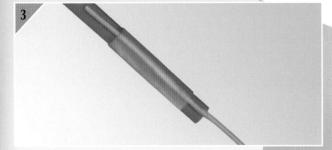

TAPE A STRAIGHTENED PAPER CLIP TO THE FREE END OF THE DRINKING STRAW. CUT AN UPRIGHT SLIT IN ONE SIDE OF THE BOX AND MARK EVENLY SPACED LINES ALONG IT. PUT THE JAR IN THE BOX, PAPER CLIP POKING THROUGH THE SLIT. BEND THE END OF THE PAPER CLIP TO MAKE A POINTER OVER THE MARKS.

WHAT YOU NEED

- jelly jar
- balloon
- drinking straw
- paper clip
- cardboard box
- tape
- scissors

CORRECT PLACE
PUT YOUR BAROMETER WHERE THE TEMPERATURE STAYS THE SAME, SUCH AS A BASEMENT. LOOK AT THE POINTER AT THE SAME TIME EACH DAY. IT SHOULD RISE AND FALL AS THE WEATHER CHANGES.

HIGHS AND LOWS

As atmospheric pressure outside increases, it compresses the air in the jar by pressing on the balloon, making the pointer rise. When atmospheric pressure falls, the jar's air pressure is now relatively higher, so it bulges the balloon and tilts the pointer down. High atmospheric pressure usually brings calm, clear weather. Low pressure often means clouds, wind, and rain.

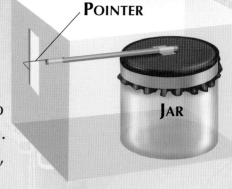

POINTER

JAR

HIGHER ATMOSPHERIC PRESSURE

LOWER ATMOSPHERIC PRESSURE

POINTER RISES

POINTER FALLS

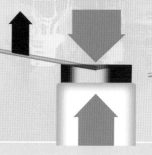

THERMOMETER

If you take your barometer from a cool place to a warm one, for a short time it becomes a thermometer instead. The heat makes the air in the jar get bigger or expand, so the pointer falls. This is why you need to keep the barometer at a constant temperature to measure the slow changes in air pressure accurately.

COOL AIR

WARM AIR

FLOATING ON AIR

As a fan or propeller turns, it pulls air in from one side and pushes it out the other. If the fan faces up, it pushes air down and provides a lifting force. The hovercraft uses this method to trap high pressure air beneath and lift itself just above the ground. It "floats on air" over land or water.

Hovercraft have lifting fans in their bodies and separate propellers to push themselves along.

PROJECT: BUILD A HOVERCRAFT

HOVERCRAFT

MAKE A HOLE WITH A PENCIL IN A SMALL SQUARE OF CARDBOARD.

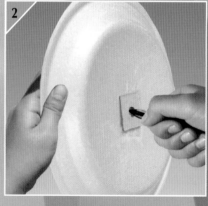

GLUE THE SQUARE TO THE POLYSTYRENE PLATE, IN THE MIDDLE OF THE BACK. PUSH A PENCIL THROUGH THE CARDBOARD HOLE AND PLATE TO MAKE A WIDER HOLE.

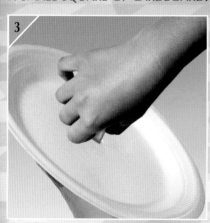

PUSH THE NECK OF THE BALLOON FROM THE BOTTOM THROUGH BOTH HOLES.

WHAT YOU NEED

- **polystyrene plate**
- **balloon**
- **cardboard**
- **glue**
- **pencil**

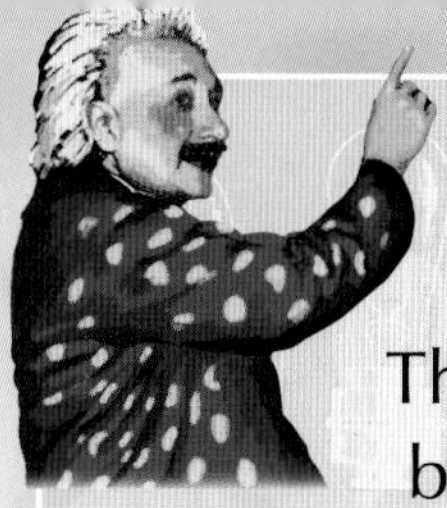

TRAPPED!

The high-pressure air rushing out of the balloon is like air being pushed down by a hovercraft's fan. It flows into the space below the plate and gets partly trapped by the plate's rim, which is like the hovercraft's flexible rubber "skirt." Air pressure rises underneath until it is enough to lift the craft slightly. As air flows out around the rim, more air rushes in from the balloon to keep up the pressure.

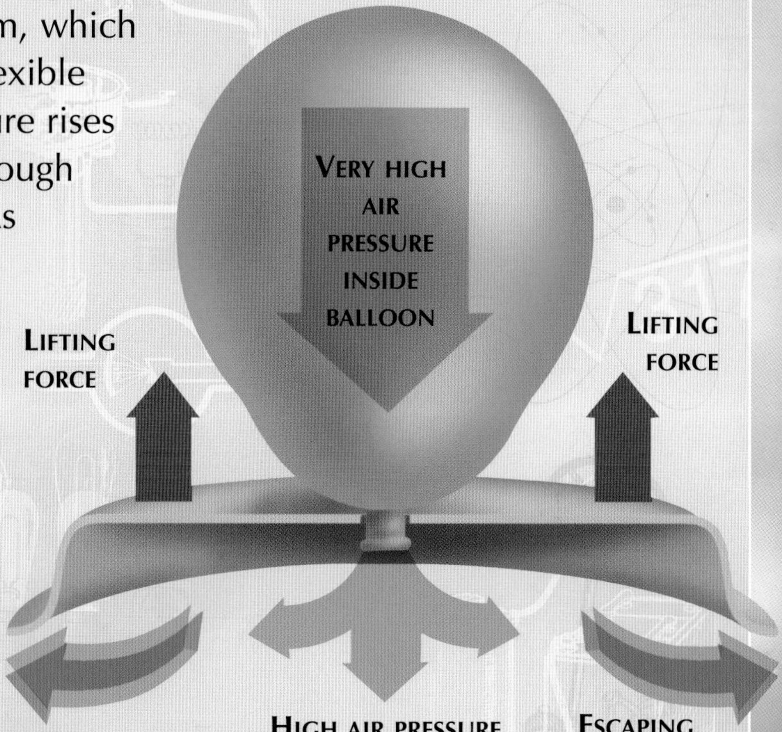

VERY HIGH AIR PRESSURE INSIDE BALLOON

LIFTING FORCE

LIFTING FORCE

ESCAPING AIR

HIGH AIR PRESSURE UNDER CRAFT

ESCAPING AIR

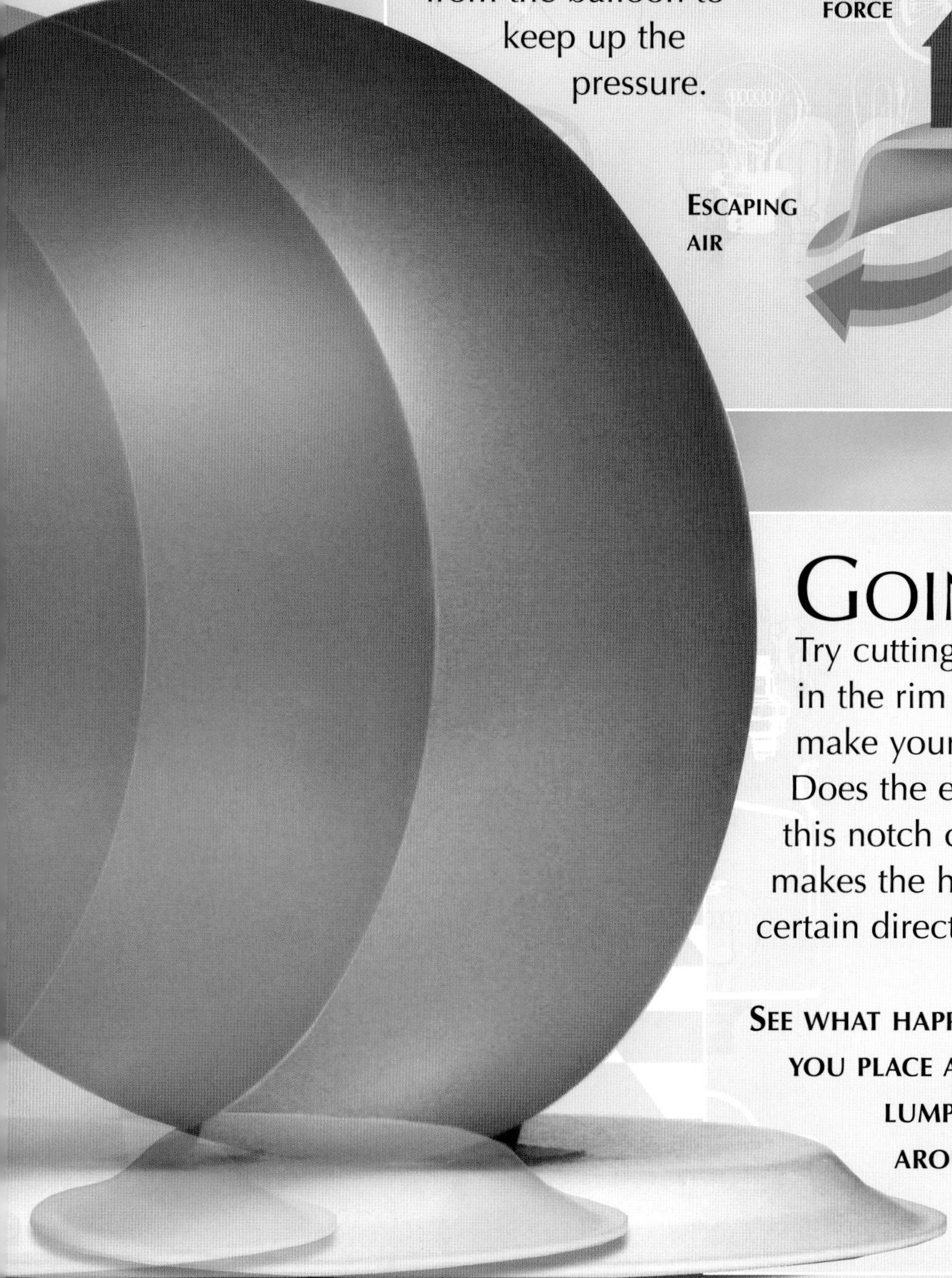

GOING FORWARD

Try cutting a small V-shaped notch in the rim of the plate, and then make your hovercraft go again. Does the extra air blowing out of this notch cause a pushing force that makes the hovercraft travel in a certain direction?

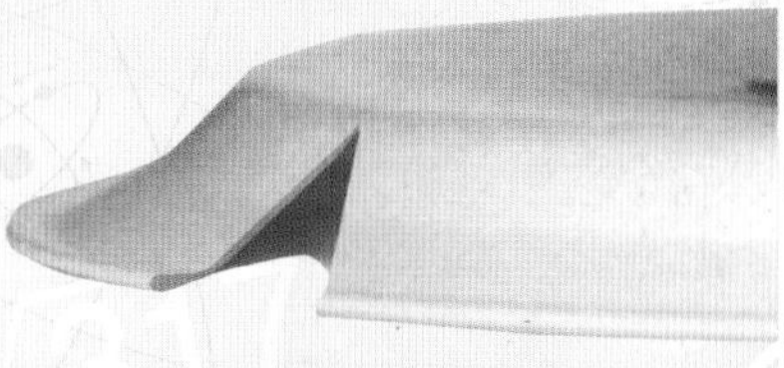

SEE WHAT HAPPENS WHEN YOU PLACE A FEW SMALL LUMPS OF MODELING CLAY EVENLY AROUND THE PLATE TO INCREASE ITS WEIGHT. DOES IT HOVER AS EASILY?

WHEN AIR PUSHES BACK

Parachutes have a large area designed to force aside lots of air. This means a large air resistance, so they drift down slowly.

As you walk along, you push air out of the way. You rarely notice, but if you run fast, you push air out of the way more quickly, and you feel this as "wind" on your face. The bigger an object is and the faster it moves, the more air it must push aside. The air pushes back with a force called air or wind resistance.

PROJECT: TEST WIND RESISTANCE

WIND TESTER

WHAT YOU NEED

- two identical toy cars
- length of stiff foam board
- two thin lengths of foam board
- paper
- tape
- electric fan
- scissors

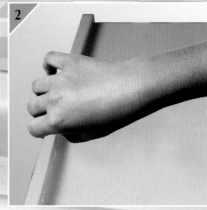

USING TWO SAME-SIZED PAPER RECTANGLES, TAPE ONE EDGE TO THE FRONT OF EACH CAR. ON ONE CAR, BEND THE PAPER TO FORM A SMOOTH CURVE. ON THE OTHER, FOLD THE PAPER INTO A FLAT FRONT. TAPE THE REAR EDGES TO THE CARS.

GLUE THIN FOAM BOARD STRIPS TO A STIFF BOARD, AS EDGES FOR THE RACETRACK. RAISE THE TRACK AT ONE END ON BOOKS FOR A GENTLE SLOPE. PLACE THE ELECTRIC FAN AT THE BOTTOM IN THE CENTER OF THE TRACK TO CREATE A "WIND."

READY SET GO!
RELEASE THE CARS FROM THE TOP OF THE SLOPE AT EXACTLY THE SAME TIME. WHICH ONE ROLLS DOWN FASTEST? (IF BOTH GATHER SPEED TOO QUICKLY, LOWER THE RAISED END OF THE BOARD TO MAKE THE SLOPE MORE SHALLOW.) SWAP THE PAPER SHAPES FROM ONE CAR TO THE OTHERS AND TEST THEM AGAIN.

WHAT A DRAG

As each car moves along, it forces its way against the air or "wind" from the fan. This air slips easily over the car with the curved paper. But it hits the car with the flat front with greater force and creates much more resistance. So this car travels slower. The slowing effect of air or wind resistance is known as drag. A smoothly widening curve that causes least drag is known as a streamlined shape.

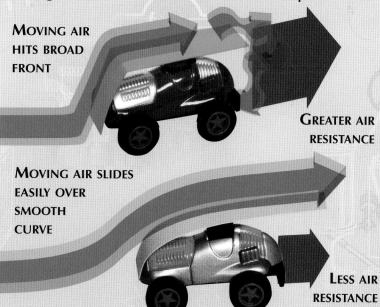

MOVING AIR HITS BROAD FRONT

GREATER AIR RESISTANCE

MOVING AIR SLIDES EASILY OVER SMOOTH CURVE

LESS AIR RESISTANCE

NOSE CONES

Try different streamlined paper shapes on the two cars, like a V or a "nose-cone."

LOOK AT THE SHAPES OF FAST CARS, BOATS, AND PLANES. SEE HOW THEY ARE STREAMLINED TO REDUCE AIR RESISTANCE OR DRAG.

How Air Flows

When designers test new shapes of cars, boats, planes, bridges, and skyscrapers, they use a wind tunnel. This blows air past the object at high speed and shows the flow by ribbons, smoke, or streamers. It helps designers create faster cars that use less fuel and structures that are safer.

Airflow over a car shows the amount of wind resistance or drag. The lower this becomes, the less fuel the car uses.

PROJECT: BUILD A WIND TUNNEL

WIND TUNNEL

WHAT YOU NEED

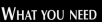

- cardboard box lid
- two stiff cardboard triangles
- four paper clips
- ribbon, or tissue paper
- thin string
- glue
- scissors
- electric fan
- cardboard tube

CUT A RECTANGLE SHAPE FROM THE MIDDLE OF THE BOX LID TO LEAVE A STRONG FRAME.

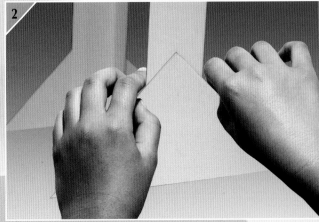

GLUE TWO LARGE CARDBOARD TRIANGLES TO THE BOTTOM OF THE SIDES, TO MAKE A FIRM BASE.

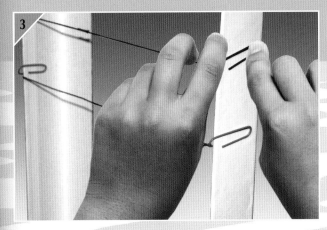

PUSH PAPER CLIPS ONTO THE FRAME EDGES. JOIN OPPOSING PAIRS OF PAPER CLIPS WITH THIN STRING STRETCHED FAIRLY TIGHT.

WRAP ONE END OF A RIBBON AROUND THE MIDDLE OF EACH STRING AND GLUE OR TAPE IT FIRMLY IN PLACE.

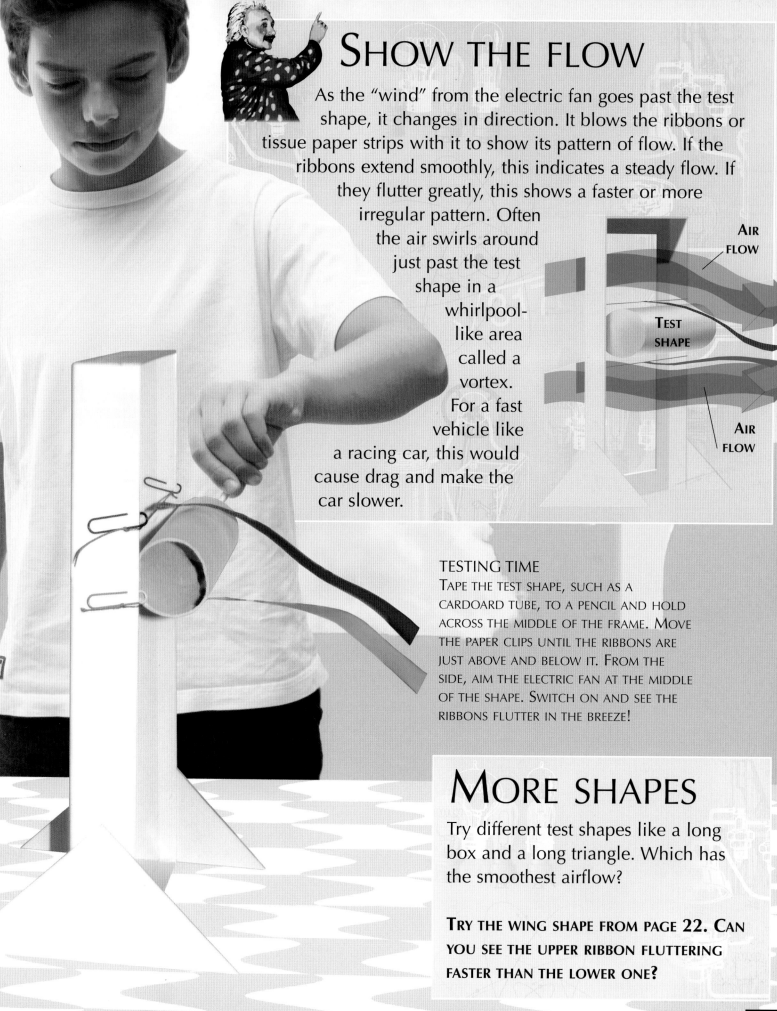

SHOW THE FLOW

As the "wind" from the electric fan goes past the test shape, it changes in direction. It blows the ribbons or tissue paper strips with it to show its pattern of flow. If the ribbons extend smoothly, this indicates a steady flow. If they flutter greatly, this shows a faster or more irregular pattern. Often the air swirls around just past the test shape in a whirlpool-like area called a vortex. For a fast vehicle like a racing car, this would cause drag and make the car slower.

AIR FLOW

TEST SHAPE

AIR FLOW

TESTING TIME

Tape the test shape, such as a cardoard tube, to a pencil and hold across the middle of the frame. Move the paper clips until the ribbons are just above and below it. From the side, aim the electric fan at the middle of the shape. Switch on and see the ribbons flutter in the breeze!

MORE SHAPES

Try different test shapes like a long box and a long triangle. Which has the smoothest airflow?

Try the wing shape from page 22. Can you see the upper ribbon fluttering faster than the lower one?

USING THE WIND

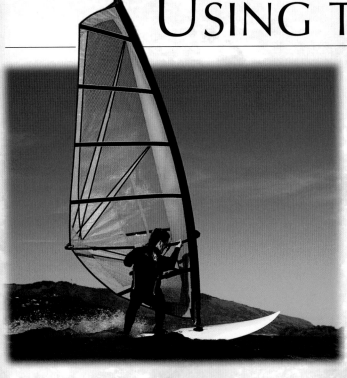

A sailboard sail has stiff strips, battens, to curve it like a plane's wing (see opposite).

Anything that moves has a type of energy known as kinetic energy. Wind is moving air. We can catch its energy to use in many ways—from sails on boats and sailboards, to wind-mills that work machines, and wind turbines that generate electricity.

PROJECT: BUILD A LANDYACHT

LANDYACHT

WHAT YOU NEED

- **foam board**
- **drinking straws**
- **thread spools**
- **paper**
- **bottle cap**
- **paper clips**
- **thread**
- **thumb tack**
- **tape**
- **glue**
- **modeling clay**
- **scissors**
- **craft knife**
- **electric fan**
- **brads**

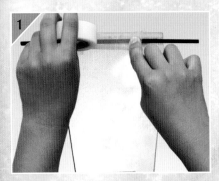

1 CUT THE YACHT'S BASE FROM FOAM BOARD. TAPE A STRAW TO THE BACK UNDERNEATH OF THE BASE FOR THE BACK AXLE.

2 STRAIGHTEN A PAPER CLIP, BEND IT IN HALF, THEN BEND THE ENDS OUTWARD TO MAKE A T. GLUE IT TO THE STRAW FOR THE BOOM.

3 TAPE THE STRAIGHT ENDS OF THE PAPER CLIP NEAR ONE END OF ANOTHER STRAW, THAT WILL BE THE MAST.

4 MAKE A SMALL HOLE IN THE MIDDLE OF THE BASE. INSERT THE LOWER END OF THE MAST. FASTEN IT UNDERNEATH WITH ANOTHER T-SHAPED PAPER CLIP.

5 CUT A TRIANGLE OF PAPER FOR THE SAIL. GLUE ONE EDGE ALONG THE MAST.

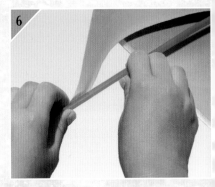

6 GLUE OR TAPE THE SAIL'S LOWER CORNER TO THE BOOM END. GIVE THE SAIL A SLIGHT CURVE.

7

PUSH A THREAD SPOOL ONTO EACH END OF THE BACK AXLE. SECURE WITH BRADS.

8

PUSH A SHORTER LENGTH OF STRAW THROUGH A THREAD SPOOL AS A FRONT AXLE. TAPE THE STRAW UNDER THE BASE BETWEEN THE FRONT FORKS. GLUE A BOTTLE CAP TO THE BACK OF THE BASE. ATTACH THREAD FROM THE BOOM END TO A THUMB TACK IN THE REAR OF THE BASE.

GONE WITH THE WIND
PUT A BALL OF MODELING CLAY INTO THE BOTTLE CAP TO WORK AS A BALLAST WEIGHT "SAILOR" AND STOP THE LANDYACHT FROM TIPPING OVER! ON A VERY SMOOTH FLOOR, USE AN ELECTRIC FAN TO BLOW THE LANDYACHT ALONG.

SAIL ON WHEELS

The "wind" from the fan pushes against the sail's large surface. This gives the sail a force in the same direction as the wind. But the landyacht cannot roll easily in this direction due to its spool wheels. However, it can use part of the force to roll forward. Experiment with different wind directions and varying the length of thread to the boom's end.

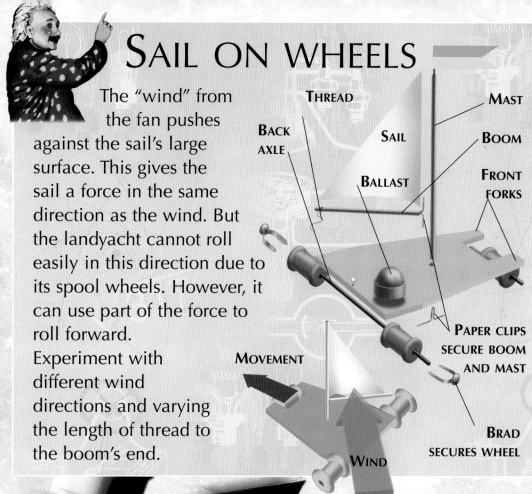

THREAD
MAST
BACK AXLE
SAIL
BOOM
BALLAST
FRONT FORKS
PAPER CLIPS SECURE BOOM AND MAST
MOVEMENT
BRAD SECURES WHEEL
WIND

AGAINST THE WIND

The sail's curved shape works like a plane wing (see next page). Wind passing over the sail creates lower air pressure in front of the sail and "sucks" in this direction. Part of this force makes the yacht roll, even into the wind, which sailors call "tacking."

TRY TO "TACK" IN A ZIG-ZAG UPWIND.

FORCE
SAIL
MOVEMENT
WIND

FLYING HIGH

Pelicans glide far without flapping, relying on their curved wing shape.

Birds, bees, and bats do it, and so do some people—fly through the air. Of course, we need planes. But a plane wing works in a similar way to a bird wing. The secret is the way that air flows over the wing's curved shape, known as an airfoil, to produce the upward force called lift.

In the late 1870s, Otto Lilienthal was first to design and fly gliders with arched airfoil-type wings.

PROJECT: BUILD A MODEL GLIDER

MODEL GLIDER

WHAT YOU NEED

- cardboard
- drinking straws
- modeling clay
- glue
- tape
- scissors

1

FOLD A LONG CARDBOARD RECTANGLE IN HALF THE LONG WAY FOR THE WING. GLUE A STRAW INTO THE FOLD. WITH THE LOWER SURFACE FLAT, PUSH THE UPPER SURFACE TO MAKE IT SLIGHTLY "HUMPED." GLUE THE EDGES.

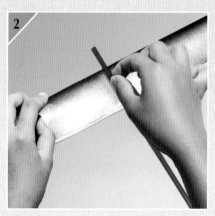

2

GLUE ANOTHER STRAW TO THE WING AT A RIGHT ANGLE. PLACE IT ON THE FLAT UNDERSIDE IN THE MIDDLE OF THE WING. MAKE SURE THE WING IS NEAR ONE END OF THE STRAW, LEAVING A SHORT "NOSE."

3

FOLD A SMALLER STRIP OF CARDBOARD IN HALF, THEN FOLD EACH OF THE HALVES IN HALF AGAIN, TO MAKE A W SHAPE. GLUE THE MIDDLE TWO SECTIONS TO MAKE THE T-SHAPED FIN (TAIL) AND REAR WINGS.

GETTING A LIFT

Air flowing past the wing must travel farther over the curved upper surface than under the flat lower surface. So this upper air moves faster and faster-moving air creates lower air pressure. The relatively higher air pressure under the wing pushes the wing and whole glider up, with a force called lift. This helps your glider to stay in the air longer.

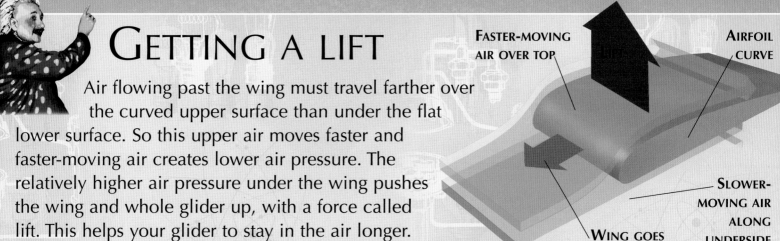

FASTER-MOVING AIR OVER TOP

AIRFOIL CURVE

SLOWER-MOVING AIR ALONG UNDERSIDE

WING GOES FORWARD

TEST FLIGHTS

YOUR CRAFT IS A GLIDER, A PLANE WITH NO ENGINE. IN WINDLESS CONDITIONS LAUNCH IT GENTLY, AIMING SLIGHTLY DOWN. IF IT NOSEDIVES, REMOVE PART OF THE COUNTERWEIGHT. IF IT SWOOPS UP AND THEN DIVES, CALLED STALLING, ADD MORE WEIGHT. KEEP ADJUSTING UNTIL THE GLIDER FLIES SMOOTHLY IN A SHALLOW DOWNWARD PATH.

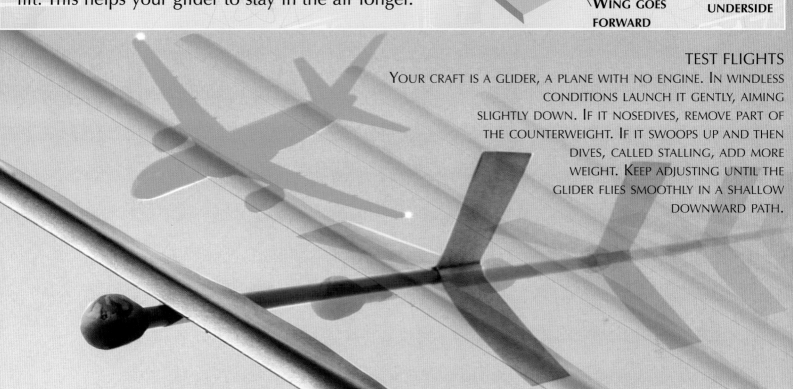

4

TAPE THE T-SHAPE TO THE LONGER END OF THE STRAW. PRESS A PIECE OF MODELING CLAY TO THE NOSE END AS A COUNTERWEIGHT, AND PREPARE FOR TAKEOFF!

SPANS AND SHAPES

Test wings of different lengths (span) and different distances from front to back (chord). Can you figure out why real gliders have very long, narrow wings? (See next page.)

LAUNCH THE GLIDER IN DIFFERENT WAYS—FAST, SLOW, SLIGHTLY UP, OR BANKED (TILTED TO ONE SIDE).

CONTROL IN THE AIR

Balloons drift with the wind. But planes can turn in different directions and climb and dive because they have moveable panels on their wings and tail called control surfaces.

The first fully controlled, powered, heavier-than-air flying machine, a plane, was the Wright brothers' *Flyer* in 1903.

PROJECT:
ADD AILERONS TO THE GLIDER

A glider has ailerons, or moveable flaps, on its wings. These help the glider to tilt, bank, and turn.

AILERONS

WHAT YOU NEED

- cardboard
- tape or glue
- scissors

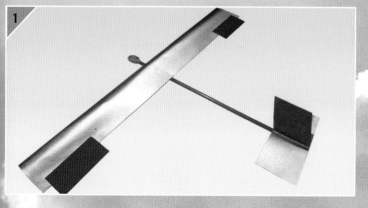

TAPE EQUAL-SIZED CARDBOARD STRIPS TO THE OUTER REAR EDGES OF THE WINGS ON YOUR GLIDER (SEE PREVIOUS PAGE).

BEND ONE OF THE AILERONS DOWN VERY SLIGHTLY AND THE OTHER ONE UP.

LIFT OR LOWER?

If the aileron angles downward, it changes the airflow over the airfoil shape and increases the force of lift. Also air coming off the bottom of the wing pushes on the aileron and forces it up. The combined effect is to raise the wing tip so the plane tilts or banks away from that side. With the aileron pointing up, the reverse happens and the wing tip is lowered.

LIFT FROM WING

MORE LIFT FROM WING

MAIN AIRFLOW

BANKING AROUND
AILERONS ARE CONTROL SURFACES AT THE REAR OF THE WING TIPS. THEY CHANGE THE FLOW OF AIR TO MAKE ONE TIP RISE AND THE OTHER FALL SLIGHTLY. THIS MAKES THE GLIDER BANK TO ONE SIDE AND SO ITS PATH TENDS TO CURVE OR TURN AROUND IN A CIRCLE. THE MORE THE AILERONS ARE ANGLED, THE STEEPER THE BANK AND THE TIGHTER THE TURN.

MORE CONTROL

Tape a cardboard strip to the rear of the glider's fin (tail). This control surface is called a rudder. With ailerons straight (not angled), bend the rudder slightly to one side and see how the glider flies.

ANGLE THE AILERON UP ON THE SIDE TO WHICH THE RUDDER IS BENT. DOES THE GLIDER TURN MORE TIGHTLY?

WINGS IN A SPIN

The forward motion of a plane's wings through the air creates lift (see previous page). Another method is to spin the wing around. It still creates lift, in the same way, but the craft does not have to move forward. This is how a helicopter flies.

Autogiros have unpowered rotors that spin in the airflow as they move forward.

The helicopter's rotors or blades are really long, thin, wings that spin around, or rotate.

PROJECT: BUILD A HELISPINNER

HELISPINNER

WHAT YOU NEED

- paper
- drinking straw
- thin dowel
- modeling clay
- glue
- tape
- scissors

MAKE TWO SMALL "HALF-WINGS" AS SHOWN ON PAGES 22–23. GLUE THEM TO ONE STRAW, FACING OPPOSITE DIRECTIONS.

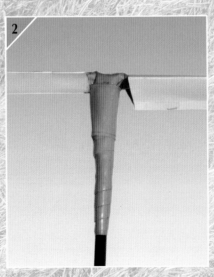

FIRMLY TAPE THE SMALL DOWEL TO THE MIDDLE OF THE STRAW.

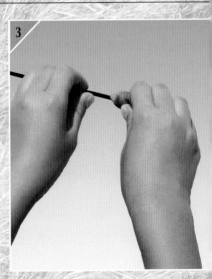

STICK A PIECE OF MODELING CLAY ONTO THE LOWER END OF THE DOWEL TO ACT AS A COUNTERWEIGHT.

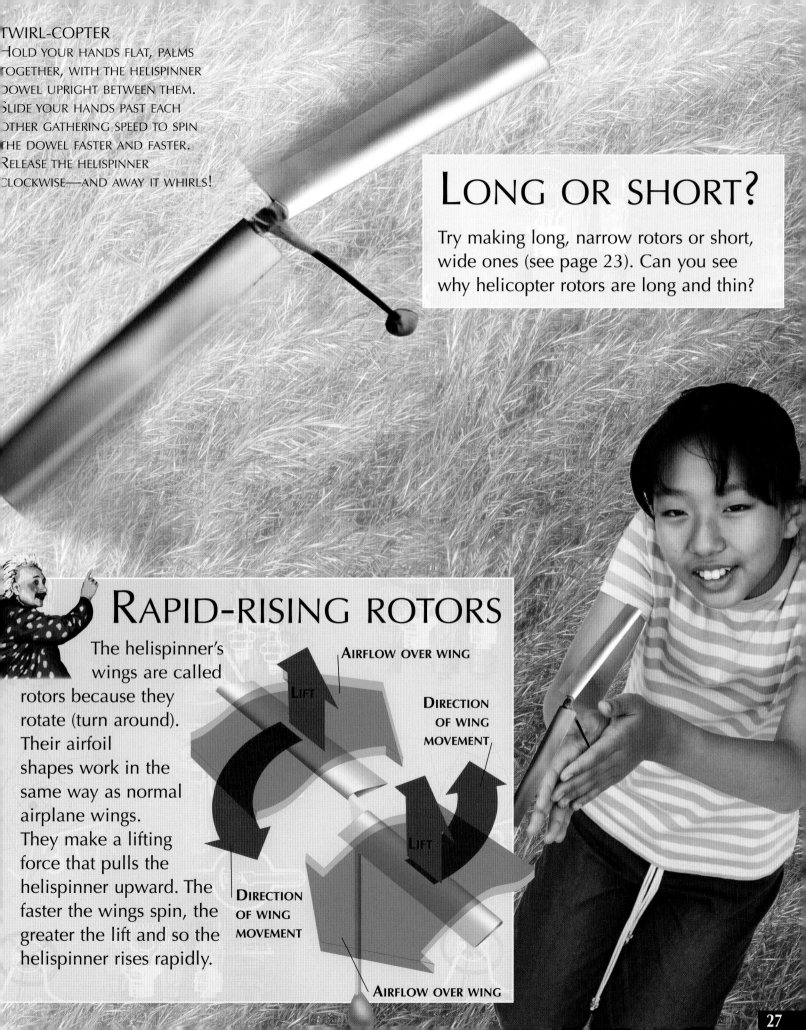

TWIRL-COPTER

Hold your hands flat, palms together, with the helispinner dowel upright between them. Slide your hands past each other gathering speed to spin the dowel faster and faster. Release the helispinner clockwise—and away it whirls!

LONG OR SHORT?

Try making long, narrow rotors or short, wide ones (see page 23). Can you see why helicopter rotors are long and thin?

RAPID-RISING ROTORS

The helispinner's wings are called rotors because they rotate (turn around). Their airfoil shapes work in the same way as normal airplane wings. They make a lifting force that pulls the helispinner upward. The faster the wings spin, the greater the lift and so the helispinner rises rapidly.

AIRFLOW OVER WING

LIFT

DIRECTION OF WING MOVEMENT

LIFT

DIRECTION OF WING MOVEMENT

AIRFLOW OVER WING

AIR, ENERGY, AND POWER

Many turbines together are known as a wind farm.

The whirling blades of wind turbines are seen on hillsides around the world. These machines change the kinetic energy of moving air (see page 20) into the energy of electricity. They help our quest for non-polluting, sustainable power.

PROJECT: BUILD A WIND TURBINE

GLUE TWO "HALF-WINGS" (SEE PAGE 26) TO A STRAW. POINT THEM THE SAME WAY, BUT WITH CURVED SURFACES OPPOSITE.

STRAIGHTEN A PAPER CLIP, BEND IT IN HALF AND THEN BEND THE ENDS TO FORM A T-SHAPE (SEE PAGE 20). TAPE THE FREE ENDS TO THE MIDDLE OF THE STRAW JOINING THE HALF-WINGS, WHICH ARE THE TURBINE BLADES.

CAREFULLY MAKE A HOLE JUST BIG ENOUGH FOR A STRAW IN THE BOTTOM OF THE PLASTIC BOTTLE AND A SIMILAR HOLE IN ITS CAP. PUSH A LONG STRAW THROUGH THE HOLES AND FIT A BEAD OVER EACH END. THIS STRAW IS THE DRIVE SHAFT.

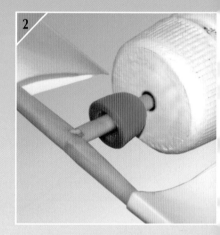

ATTACH THE BLADES TO THE SHAFT BY GLUING THE CENTRAL PART OF THE PAPER CLIP INTO THE END OF THE STRAW AT THE CAP.

WHAT YOU NEED

- **plastic bottle**
- **cardboard tube**
- **thin/thick cardboard**
- **drinking straws**
- **thick card**
- **beads**
- **paper clips**
- **string**
- **glue**
- **tape**
- **scissors**

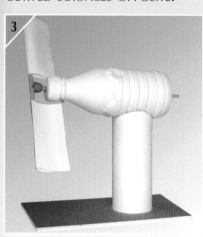

MAKE A TALL TUBE TOWER AND WIDE BASE FROM CARDBOARD. TRIM THE TUBE TOP TO FIT THE PLASTIC BOTTLE AND GLUE IT ON.

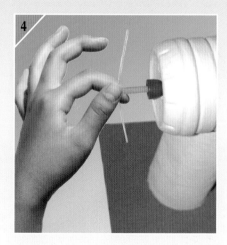

BEND ANOTHER PAPER CLIP INTO A T-SHAPE. GLUE THIS INTO THE OTHER END OF THE SHAFT.

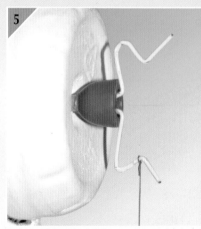

BEND THE PAPER CLIP'S ENDS INTO V-SHAPED HOOKS. TIE ONE END OF THE STRING TO ONE V AND THE OTHER END TO A BEAD.

WIND WORK

The rotor blades of the turbine work like plane wings, each creating a lifting force at its curved surface. This force does not actually lift the blade. It "sucks" it around in a circle making the drive shaft turn. The two rotor blades work together since their curved surfaces face opposite ways so their lifting forces give the same turning motion.

CURVED SURFACE FACES DOWN

DRIVE SHAFT SPINS

AIRFLOW

LIFT

WEIGHT RISES

TOWER

AIRFLOW

BASE

CURVED SURFACE FACES UP

WHEN WIND WINDS

PLACE THE WIND TURBINE IN A WINDY PLACE OR BLOW AN ELECTRIC FAN AT IT. (PUT WEIGHTS ON THE BASE IF NEEDED TO HOLD IT STILL.) THE BLADES BEGIN TO WHIRL AND TURN THE DRIVE SHAFT. THIS WINDS THE STRING AROUND THE HOOKS AND RAISES THE BEAD. THE WIND'S ENERGY IS MADE INTO TURNING ENERGY, WHICH IS USED TO LIFT THE BEAD WEIGHT.

BLADE SHAPES

Try making another set of rotors, but this time glue them at angle to each other on the straw, like the blades of a fan. Is this version of the turbine more powerful?

FOR THESE ANGLED ROTORS, DOES IT MATTER IF THE CURVED (AIRFOIL) SURFACE OF EACH BLADE FACES FORWARD OR THE FLAT SURFACE?

HISTORY OF AIR

About 520 B.C.E. In ancient Greece, scientist and thinker Anaximenes suggested that air was a "primary substance" which could be turned into other substances and materials.

335 B.C.E. Aristotle described how air was one of the four "elements" from which all other substances and materials were made, the other three being fire, water, and earth. These views lasted almost 2,000 years.

1620 Jan Baptista van Helmont suspected that air was not a single pure substance but a mixture of different substances that he named gases.

1643 Evangelista Torricelli made an early version of the barometer and said that air was a real substance with weight.

1674 John Mayow reported that a candle in a sealed jar used up part of the air as it burned and a mouse in the jar did the same. He stated that air contained "nitro-arial spirit" needed for burning and breathing.

1772 Several scientists, including Karl Scheele, discovered a gas in air which was later called nitrogen.

1774 Joseph Priestly discovered a gas that made a candle burn extra-bright. He told colleague Antoine Lavoisier, who figured out that air was one-fifth oxygen, needed for burning, and breathing, and four-fifths "azote" ("no life"), later renamed nitrogen.

1783 Joseph-Michael and Jacques-Etienne Montgolfier made the first hot air balloon. Later that year Jean Pilatre de Rozier and Francois Laurent (Marquis d'Arlandes) made the first balloon flight.

1884 Sir James Dewar showed how air could be turned into a liquid, following research by Szygmunt Wroblewski and Karol Olszewski.

1890s William Ramsay proved that air contained tiny amounts of other gases. We now know these are argon, helium, krypton, xenon, neon, and radon.

1902 The first practical airship and the first air conditioner were made.

1903 Orville Wright made the first true airplane flight in the *Flyer* designed and built by him and his brother Wilbur.

1985 Scientists first measured loss of ozone (O_3), a form of oxygen in air that led to the "ozone hole" in the atmosphere allowing the sun's harmful radiation through.

GLOSSARY

Anemometer device that measures the speed of wind

Atmosphere layer of air around earth that becomes less dense with height

Atom smallest piece or particle of a pure substance (chemical element)

Barometer device that measures the pressure of air

Density amount of matter of a substance, usually measured as mass or weight, in a certain volume

Drag force pushing against an object as it travels through a fluid, as when air pushes back on a car

Fluid substance that can flow, including liquids like water and gases like those in air

Gas substance that can flow and change volume to fill its container completely

Isobar line on a weather map that joins places of equal atmospheric pressure

Kinetic energy energy possessed by an object or substance due to its having movement or motion

Lift force created by the wing shape called the airfoil that lifts a plane upward

Meteorology study of the atmosphere, especially the processes and events of weather and climate

Molecules two or more atoms joined together to make the smallest pieces or particles of most everyday substances and materials

Pressure pushing or pressing force measured over a certain area

Thermometer device that measures temperature or the amount of heat energy in a substance or object

Wind resistance force pushing against an object that tries to move through air or against the wind

Wind vane broad surface that can swivel around showing the direction the wind blows

INDEX